DINING OUT

HOW TO OPERATE A
PROFITABLE RESTAURANT
and Keep Your Customers Coming Back

Sharon Suffolk

DINING OUT

DINING OUT: How to Operate a Profitable Restaurant and Keep Your Customers Coming Back

Copyright © 2016 by Sharon Suffolk

Published by Pacelli Publishing
9905 Lake Washington Blvd. NE, #D-103
Bellevue, Washington 98004
PacelliPublishing.com

ISBN-10: 1-933750-48-0
ISBN-13: 978-1-933750-48-4

Introduction

How to operate a successful restaurant? You might say, "It's easy, I'm doing it right now." Really? So many owners have their heads in the sand. They are blinded by the everyday, mundane chores, duties, and obligations that it's difficult to see what is happening around them.

You say, "I have plenty of customers. Even some repeats." The sad thing is, they come because you offer the best of the worst in most cases. They will settle for less than adequate food rather than drive to another town for *great* food or *great* service. I'm one of those customers who has been settling for mediocre food and service so that I don't have to drive ten or fifteen miles for dinner. However, I'm to the point that I no longer can do this without speaking out.

Thus the purpose of this book. With over fifty years of experience as a waitress, bartender, and gourmet cook, along with traveling the world and dining in the finest of eateries, I feel that I owe it to you to publish this book. I hope it will make a difference.

Contents

1

Welcome to my Place

I decided to write this book in hopes that what you are reading will make some sense to you and will motivate you to change your mode of operation. Many times it's just a few adjustments to the building, the interior, the staff or the menu. In some cases, it's all of these. Take the time periodically to analyze your "home away from home." Most likely, you are there more than you are at home.

In this book, I'm going to share with you some very important things that will make your restaurant a better place to dine--an enjoyable place with great food and amazing service. Plus, a profit center. Of course, your first thought is, "How? I have a great place now. What can I change that would make things better?"

It doesn't matter what you are serving. It does matter how it's done. You are probably saying, "I have a great staff." Think again. There's more to a business than having decent food and someone to serve it. I have been to some extremely old establishments that had great food, but the atmosphere was so bad I chose to never go back. I've been to some elegant ones that had terrible food. Getting it right isn't that hard. What is hard is keeping it going in the right direction.

There are so many types of restaurants:

Fast food
Cafeteria/Buffet
Food truck
Sports Bar/Grill
Food themed
Children's play and pizza place
Airport bar/grill
Diners (we use to call them truck stops)
Family style without alcohol
Family style with alcohol
Casual dining
Outdoor dining
Fine dining

DINING OUT

What type of business do you own? It matters when you are reading this book and how you approach the changes. Depending on the type of establishment, certain standards are acceptable or expected. However, some basic principles still apply. All of these standards have the same things in common. Good food, cleanliness, good service and hopefully good prices.

I'm frustrated with the journey of trying to find a good restaurant. It never fails that one time it's great, then next time it's a disaster of sorts. Maybe the staff is having a bad night because they are having personal issues, maybe the chef is in a bad mood because the fish or meat he ordered isn't as good as expected. Personally, I don't want to be the recipient of their frustration. I don't need to know that there are problems. I want to enjoy my time away from my own kitchen.

I enjoy a good meal. Even more, I LOVE good service. My goal is to improve every bar, grill, diner, fast food, slow food or whatever you want to call your business. Ambitious goal? Maybe, but I'm going to try.

I hope you are now getting the point that there's more to this picture.

Welcome to my home

When you think of your home, what do you think? Is it clean? Tidy? Organized? Is your family friendly? Well groomed? What's your opinion on how others view your home? Think of it as if your house is for sale. Is it clean and as neat outside as in? Does it have curb appeal? Why should someone want to come in?

It's the same thing with your restaurant--it's your "house and family" that make the first impression. Start with the outside and work your way in. Who is the first person your customer sees when they enter the door? Are your guests greeted by a hostess or staff member who is excited to be working, or one who doesn't care if they are there or not? Are they neatly dressed? If you have a hostess stand, is it clear of clutter?

The person who greets your guests needs to have a smile on their face, be nicely dressed, and have a friendly attitude. This is worth repeating. They say a smile can change a bad situation into an amazing one. Make sure everyone has their smile on.

Greeting your customer starts the journey. If I walk into a restaurant and the wait staff isn't friendly, you can bet it throws up a red flag. I didn't go out to eat to have a bad time. I want to have an enjoyable meal and experience. That doesn't mean they are there to entertain me, but I sure don't need them to bring me down to their bad mood.

DINING OUT

2

The Outside

Why do NEW consumers choose one place over another? It's pretty obvious. The outside of your business is the deciding factor on whether or not customers come in for the first time or go on by.

In this crazy world of accepting mediocrity, there is still no valid excuse for dirty entrances, rain streaked windows, torn awnings or stale cigarette butts at the door. Healthy, happy people want a pleasant experience entering a restaurant. One that has a filthy entrance gives worry. What is the rest of the place like? Will I get sick if I eat here? Will this food even be edible? Just a few thoughts that go through customers' minds when seeing an unkempt entrance. They may get a wrong impression of your entire operation.

Step back. Step outside. Look at it as if you had never been in this area. Take an honest look at every inch of the building, grounds, signs and other surroundings. Do you need all of the posters in the windows? Would a fresh coat of paint help? It doesn't need to look like the entrance of a 5-star restaurant but it should be clean and inviting. Would you take a chance on eating here? Would you bring your family here? Would you recommend it from just the outside appearance? Be honest. Ask others for their opinion. Most of all, listen to what is being said or not said from customers who never come back.

For many years, we drove by a small, roadside restaurant in a very tiny Northern Michigan town. It wasn't anything fancy. It was however, inviting. Much to our surprise, when we did stop there, it was just as warm, cozy and inviting inside as it was outside. The extra bonus was the amazing, home-cooked food and friendly, intelligent, and well-groomed wait staff.

What does inviting have to do with the operations of a good restaurant? It's simple. If the outside doesn't appeal or invite you in, then you need to ask yourself the tough questions, "Why isn't this placed packed tonight?" What will bring in the new customers?" Why isn't the local community supporting my business?" Good questions that you need to think about and act on.

New customers don't always have the luxury of hearing a recommendation from a friend or family member. They might be new to the community. They might be in town just for the day but you still want and need them to choose your restaurant over the one down the street. Local residents do rely on referrals and eye appeal. Just like when you meet a new person, your first impression is usually your lasting one.

Remember when you first pulled into the parking lot? What did you think about the property? What was your first impression? Clean, inviting, pleasant, warm and friendly? Or dirty, cold, grimy, dark, dingy and old? Remember what you wanted to do when you first started the planning stages of how you imagined it would look? Did you achieve that goal? Are you keeping up with that dream place? Be real with your thoughts. Don't fool yourself. You may not be fooling your customers.

If the outside of your establishment, whether a building or a food truck, is dirty, cluttered or just plain tired looking, it doesn't matter what the inside is like. You take pride in what your serve. You take pride in your inside décor, so why not the outside? Even if you don't own the building you MUST make it inviting.

Coming into the building

The last thing that a customer wants to see is a dirty entrance. That would trigger the signal that the rest of the restaurant is just as dirty. Cockroaches, bugs, germs, spoiled food or worse. You can mask some of the dirt, but anyone knows that it is there. Why would they continue inside? I will NEVER eat at a place where the outside looks like a war zone or dumping station. And I'd bet you wouldn't either.

Consider your exterior décor. Just because you are in Florida you don't have to decorate with flamingos. Or if you are in Minnesota you don't need bears and elk at the door--unless that's what you serve. Get the point?

Take a few minutes and walk around your building. Remove yourself from the business and ask yourself what you really see. Do you see a clean entrance? Do you see sparkling windows? Flowers, plants or maybe a bench for waiting? Do this often. Don't get complacent.

Is your parking lot in good condition? Is it well marked? Do you have potholes? Fix the problems. It's part of the picture.

Are your windows used as advertisements for out-of-date community events? It's fine to have an uncluttered, maintained and current bulletin board area, but keep the windows clean and free of clutter and posters or flyers.

What about your signs? Do they have burned out light bulbs or missing letters? Do they show that you are open for business? A poorly kept sign says that you aren't making enough money to make repairs or that you don't care about what the customer thinks. I can't imagine owning and operating a business where first impressions are so important and not paying attention to every part.

You may and should worry about the appearance of your staff and the food presentation. But start from the outside and work your way in, or you may not have any business on the inside.

Back to the Northern Michigan restaurant. It's one of the places that we go out of our way to visit every time we go north. Why? Because it is always neat and clean and the food is consistently good. No clutter at the door. No trash cans sitting around by the entrance. The windows are clean. Fresh flowers grow around the perimeter. It's just plain inviting. Year after year after year. Honestly, we time our trips so that we can stop for a good home cooked meal served by a great staff.

3

The Entrance

Ok so you see what you need to do with the outside, now let's talk about the next step--the entry. Once again, this is a first impression thing. The outside of the building was good enough to get me inside. Now I will think either, "This place is not what I expected," or "WOW!"

You may have entered a business expecting a certain look and been disappointed. I want your customers to be pleased that they chose your place to dine.

The most important part of the initial visit from a new customer or one of your regulars is the entry. I can't emphasize this enough that this is the doorway to your home. This is the doorway to your success. Your doorway makes or breaks you in more ways than you think. A dirty, dingy entrance sets the tone for what your customers think about you, your business and its operations.

Sweep your doorway every day. And I mean sweep it. A clean house is important and the doorway is a part of the house. Steam clean carpets frequently. Steam clean the tile floors frequently. Get in the corners! Keep the entrance to your restaurant as clean as the rest of the building. Customers notice how every part of the building is kept. It shows your pride.

This is quite often where the overflow has to wait when you have a full house. What are they doing while waiting? Looking around. I notice the floors and windows. If the corners are nasty and the windows are dirty, I am more inclined to leave. I don't want to see the rest of the place. I don't want to think about how the food is being prepared. I am very serious about the entry being clean.

One of the obvious things is to NOT allow customers to smoke or put out their cigarettes at your doorway. No one wants to smell stale cigarettes as they enter the door. If you have a designated area for those who smoke outside, make sure it is at least 30 feet from the door or in an area where others do not have to pass through.

If your entry is large enough for furniture, make sure that it is clean and inviting. Sometimes just a freshly painted wooden bench is all you need. Stay away from upholstered furniture unless you are willing and able to clean it frequently. A dirty chair or couch is something that your customers notice.

Make sure your entrance has a pleasant fragrance. A vase of fresh flowers is always a wonderful and welcoming thing to have on a table. If you don't have room, then an air freshener works. Lavender is a fragrance that calms the nerves and can create an atmosphere and feeling of contentment upon entering your establishment.

For the safety of your customers, always maintain the entry. Never have rugs that keep kicking up and become a hazard. Make sure your floors are dry and not slippery. The grease from the kitchen penetrates through the air and can cause a slippery floor throughout the entire building. Use safety mats or removable carpets. Clean the carpets and mats daily. And don't forget the windows or glass doors. A dirty door is a sign that the rest of the house is unkempt.

4

Inside Your House

Now that I'm inside the "house," I have been met by a pleasant staff and am being taken to my table or booth. What's next? Look around the room. What catches your eye? What makes you want to stay? Or not. Think about it.

I'm going to say this again, the interior continues to tell the story of how you feel about your business. Whether it's inside or out. If it looks bad, it confirms that your business is down. It confirms that you don't care about your clientele. It confirms that you don't care about anything but getting through the day.

It is easy to say that you don't have enough time to take care of the day-to-day chores. But take the time now to look around. Are your walls clean? Do they need a fresh coat of paint or to be washed? Do they complement the rest of the room? Do you have Italian furniture, Early American wall decorations, Western bar stools, Turkish rugs and Aunt Mary's favorite table? Do you have a mixture of tables and chairs? Does it look like a pawn shop more than a well thought-out environment? Decorate like you would your home. Decorate with one clean and updated theme.

Do your tables look like they did the day they were purchased? Are they in need of some repairs? How are the chairs? Check out the furniture. Fix the wobbly chair. Fix the tear on the seat of the booth. Polish the wood tables. Are they all clean and in good repair? Get the picture? Touch and feel all of the edges to make sure that your cleaning staff is taking the time that you require. Show them where they need to spend more time. Set a routine maintenance schedule for the entire room. Have a checklist posted.

What about the floor? Is the carpet clean and not worn? If you have tile, how are you keeping it fresh? Dirty grout is disgusting. Stained carpet shouts "FILTH." It is a never-ending but necessary task to keep the floors clean and fresh. Look under the tables and booths. Move the tables and chairs when you sweep or clean. Never leave debris in the corners.

It's acceptable to sweep the floors or carpets as long as you are not creating a dust storm. NEVER vacuum when you have guests in the house. Everyone appreciates not having to walk through crumbs or spills. Keep up the floors is really a challenge but can be done tastefully.

With all the cleaning tools and products on the market today, I cannot find one excuse to not have clean floors. I wouldn't want to eat in a place where they don't clean the tables properly. I will not eat in a place where they don't clean the floors properly.

Are the window sills cleaned daily? Why not? Keep this area as clean as your tables and floors. And not when your customers are in the building!

Can you see out of the windows? Am I being flippant? No, I'm being very serious. This is as much of a deterrent as a dirty floor. Dirty windows and blinds are disgusting. Dust floats through the air and on to the tables and food. Keep these areas as clean as the other parts of the room.

5

The Table

N ow comes another one of my biggest gripes when it comes to the inside--the table setting.

At home, it's easy to set a proper table. Keeping the table surface clean isn't a daunting chore. You use proper cleaning tools and products. You want to keep your family healthy. You would never ask them to eat off of a germ ridden, greasy, or sticky table. So why do you expect your customers to do it?

I am constantly amazed at the way restaurant owners think that using the same dirty rag that was sitting in a filthy water bucket is actually cleaning a table properly. If you would send a water sample to a lab, the results would be astonishing. GERMS, GERMS, and more GERMS. The health department would and should shut you down.

And you want your customer to put their spoon or fork directly on that surface. Think again.

Even if you put chemicals in that bucket, the germs are still on the rag. Yes, it costs a little more but use a spray bottle with a mixture of water and a disinfectant to clean the table surface. Next, use a clean rag for each table and never wipe the seats with the rag then again the table. How disgusting is this habit? People just sat there. They might as well have been sitting on the table. Whatever it takes, do it. It's worth every penny and minute.

I was in a Coney Island style restaurant recently. It was midmorning. My friend and I were having a pleasant breakfast and lingering over our coffee when I noticed that the busboy was climbing on the booth seats to clean the dirty windows and blinds. Really! What in the world were the owners thinking? Why would they clean these areas when a customer was in the next booth and not have it done while the restaurant is closed for the night? Howard Johnson was turning over in his grave.

This was so disturbing to me. There's a place and time for everything and this definitely was neither of those. The dust was flying everywhere and coming my way. Thank goodness we were ready to leave.

Now I'm wondering about how they clean the kitchen. Or do they? The dishes look clean, but if they are stored in an area where the staff wipes the shelves with a dirty rag or dusts near the stack, I wondered, what else I was eating on my plate.

I should have said something at that moment but felt that it might embarrass my friend. We talked about it outside and agreed that it was improper. Now I'm sorry that I didn't take the time to at least express my concern and thoughts. This is another one of those "I won't go back" places even though the food is good. The worst part about this is that the owner doesn't know why I'm not coming back. Or why I'm not recommending this restaurant.

Setting the Table

Presentation of the table setting is so important. It tells your customer that you really want them to enjoy their meal as much as the presentation of their food.

I know the new trend is to go "green," but not in the table settings, unless your theme is green. What I mean is don't scrimp on this area. Use either table linens or place mats. Even if you are operating a diner with fast turnover, show your customer that you care about their health and well-being. Paper placemats are a must, as well as a napkin.

Be creative. If you have a western or country theme going on, use paper towels. How fun would that be? If you're operating a family style restaurant, use colorful ones that would cheer up everyone. Linen is always expected in a finer element.

Do you have outdoor dining? This is the most relaxing way to enjoy a meal. Nothing is better than sitting outside and enjoying the pleasant weather. However, when sitting down at a patio environment, I try not to think about what was just on my table. A bird, a squirrel, flies or worse. This of all places requires placemats or linens. I will not touch the table with my utensils. Would you?

You might be saying that it's not cost efficient to use placemats. You'd need to make sure you have stock, store them and consider the extra trash they create. My feeling is that if you really care about the cleanliness of your tables and the peace of mind that your customers have with eating at a clean table, you'll find that these things are far less complicated than you think.

What might surprise you more is that your customer will recommend your place to others because of the cleanliness. Customers equal money.

Is asking for clean matching decent grade silverware too much? Mismatched, cheap, bent, dirty silverware is unacceptable. Oh, and what about serving a dinner on chipped dishes? Oh yes, we've had that experience in a local restaurant recently. Both my husband's and my dishes were chipped and the silverware was dirty. I could write a book on this restaurant alone! It shouldn't be in business. Am I describing your place?

6

The Staff - Impressions

Now it's time to talk about your staff. And YOU. Do you require uniforms for your staff? Do you frequently check them to make sure that they are wearing neat, clean items? Do you notice when workers look tired or ill? YOU NEED TO! Your customer notices all of this.

What about your appearance? Rhea, an owner of a local 3-star restaurant, always looks tired and is in clothing that is wrinkled and two sizes too small for her large frame. She needs a makeover. I know it's a tiring job but there's no reason to present yourself looking like a billboard that says, "I'm Tired, "I'm Worn Out," or "I Need a Vacation." Take a hard look in the mirror each morning.

Take some time to take care of yourself and your appearance. YOU ARE THE COMPANY.

Back to your staff. It isn't necessary to wear a uniform. Clean clothes are necessary. A neat, clean wait person is essential to your business. Dirty clothing tells me that they don't care about themselves, so why would they care about your business? This includes the bus boys, the kitchen crew, the bar staff and anyone else you have working for you.

Consider a dress code. This way, everyone knows what to wear. It makes it easy. A white shirt and black slacks. All black. Blue shirt with beige slacks. Whatever color combination you choose, it vilifies that you care about your customer and what they think about you.

One of my pet peeves is body piercings. Unless you are running a really low-class joint, dump the piercings. Don't allow your employees to come to work with rings in their nose, tongue, lip or other unusual places. It's unnecessary and unsanitary.

One time we were traveling and stopped at what we thought would be a nice, clean family-style food place to get a good bowl of soup and a cup of coffee. I don't remember the place but I do remember that the waitress could hardly talk because she had her tongue pierced and a ring which showed her teeth in her lower lip/jaw area. Really. I wasn't expecting this. I couldn't eat my food because of the appearance of the waitress. I'll leave this up to you if you accept it. It depends on the type of business you are running whether or not this is acceptable. But I don't think piercings are a wise thing to allow. I don't care how good-looking the person might be, rings should only be on fingers.

Hair—No, I'm not talking about the Broadway musical. I'm talking about real hair. The stuff on your staff's head. And it should stay on the head. Hair should never be in my soup. I don't want to share the flavor of hair spray with the spices of my food. I will not eat food served to me if the wait staff's hair has been touching it. Many restaurants, for good reason, require that the hair be neat and out of the face. Make sure the hair is contained and NOT in the food.

It doesn't matter if you are running a food tent on a beach or a 5-star reservation-only food establishment. If the staff looks shabby or unkempt, it will be reflected on the entire company.

The tone the staff sets is so important. They represent you! If they are happy in their position it will be reflected in their performance. I was recently at a country club in a small town in northern Michigan having dinner with friends when our waiter started to tell us his story of how miserable he was working for the new owner. How overwhelmed he was, had worked too many hours that week and was tired. He had to do duties that he felt wasn't in the job description. Really? He actually asked us to wait until he waited on two other tables that came in after us because they were not as friendly as us and his boss would not like it if they had to wait for their dinners. Unbelievable. The food was pricey but very well prepared. Did that matter? Not at that point, after waiting for over an hour for it to arrive and be inaccurate. Needless to say, we will think about it before we go back, even though it is an amazing facility. I don't need to be a social worker while out to dinner.

So many times I have been angry because the wait staff made me feel that they were being "bothered" by having to wait on me instead of grateful to have a job. I love an enthusiastic, friendly but not overboard service provider. It's not comfortable to be in a situation where the person waiting on you is not happy to be doing their job. I have worked with so many people over the years who were really attractive, well groomed, and educated, but extremely unhappy in their jobs and it came through loud and clear. It actually made me look at them differently.

Now turn this around. I'll call her Sheila. Sheila wasn't the most beautiful woman, she had mousey brown hair that need a good cut, fair skin, was in her fifties and overweight. BUT when she approached our table—WOW--she was amazing. Her bubbly spirit was infectious. No one even noticed her weight or hair style. She was neatly groomed. She obviously loved her job. She was articulate. She knew the menu and how to explain each item. She spoke highly of the establishment, the food and her boss. She was on her game. Our concerns about eating there were gone.

One of our better experiences was with a restaurant in Bonita Springs, Florida. We have been there several times over the past couple of years and never have been disappointed by the building condition, the host staff, the wait staff or their amazing food. How do they do it year after year? Simple--the owners are there every day and care about what is going on. They care about their staff, but more importantly, their customers. The only issue that we had to endure was being called "Honey" or

"Sweetie." It may be a Southern tradition but I'd still rather they dropped it. The restaurant is one of the favorites of our friends who winter in that area. It has been recommended by so many for good reasons. We'll go back next time we're there for sure.

I love people who smile. Oh, those pearly whites! A smile can hide so many emotions. But a real smile is a gift. Not everyone has pearly whites. In my case, even though my teeth are slightly discolored, I still have a happy smile. I've been told that I have a "happy" face. My eyes smile. Smiles come from within. It's hard for everyone to have an honest, heartfelt smile all the time but when you are in the retail business, it's a must.

You don't surround yourself at your home with Debbie Downers. You don't like to spend time with people who are not happy, healthy, clean, and articulate. Why do you expect your customers to spend time with staff that isn't?

Think of your staff as family. If it were your family would you want them to dress or look any differently. Be proud of who represents you. Regardless of the gender, age or size of the employee, require that they keep up a clean and healthy appearance. More on staff training in the next chapter.

7

The Staff - Training.

I have been a waitress. I have been a bartender. I've been a hostess. I have worked the long hard hours. I have put up with nasty customers. I tolerated rude, inconsiderate, and lazy coworkers. I have heard the tirades of the chef and the ranting of the bosses. What haven't I heard or experienced? Not much.

I worked in many different types of food establishments for the same reasons your staff works for you--to make a living. And I made a good living. I also sold to the restaurants for many years.

I started working as a waitress at Howard Johnsons on the Ohio Turnpike at the age of 18, and have told the following story many times.

I feel, no, I KNOW that the training I received at HoJo's was without a doubt the best in the industry. I only wish that they had printed a manual that would be available today. Howard and the rest of the staff had it right. No-nonsense service. No-nonsense manners. No-nonsense appearance. No nonsense period. The management had a policy about how they wanted everything done from the how you tied your apron bow to how and when you left the building at the end of your shift. Their no-nonsense policies were known when you interviewed for the job and you were reminded of them constantly while employed there. If you didn't like their rules, you were not so pleasantly asked to work elsewhere.

Personally, I found that their rules were so close to my personality and the way I wanted to be treated as a customer that I actually applauded them for making sure that everyone adhered to them. When I was working for this company, I was proud of my job, myself and my accomplishments for the day. It was easy to serve a customer with a smile, a kind remark and perfect delivery of their order. It didn't matter if they ordered a cup of coffee or a full meal. Everyone was treated equally--with respect and courtesy.

The many things I was taught there have carried on with me throughout my life. I didn't really need someone to teach me how to work hard, that part came naturally. I didn't need them to show me that treating others like you would like to be treated makes a difference. What I did need to hear was that it all pays off and others want the same thing.

I have also worked in local restaurants where the work ethics weren't so strict but the same rules applied--be considerate of the person who is there as your customer. Make sure they feel important and appreciated. Make sure they leave with a smile on their face.

I want to touch on a few of the areas where your staff can improve. O.K., you think you have the best of the best working with you. Think again. If that were the case, you wouldn't need this book.

When you think of your staff, start with the first person your customer sees when they enter the door. Is there a hostess or a wait-staff member who doesn't care if they are there or not? Make sure it is someone who is smiling and nicely dressed with a friendly attitude.

What about the service? Or lack of.
This is one of the things that really separates a place with a good meal and a place with an "I'll never go there again" meal.

Right from the start, training is important. Re-training is even more important. Not everyone you hire is experienced. Even if they worked at another similar place, it doesn't mean they know how to properly serve a meal. The easiest way to have them show you is to "be the customer." Sit down and let them serve you a meal. Have then serve a secret diner. Take notes. Work with them on the areas they need to improve. Compliment them on the areas where they excel. Everyone loves a compliment. Share their techniques with others.

One more first impression. Quite often I've noticed that a waitress or waiter introduces themselves to the customer. This is a great way to reach out to your customer and let them know that you really care about them. But don't let that caring stop there.

After the initial "Hello, I'm _____, may I get you something to start off your meal?" it is extremely rude for the waitress to ask the male at the table what he would like before the asking the women. I know that the days of

44

chivalry are gone, when the male would order for the female. But still, we are not beyond respecting the female and asking for her order first. This mistake happens at almost every place we go.

Does your staff write down orders? Do they make a mental note about what customer ordered what? Do they take the extra steps to make sure the customer knows about any drink or food specials of the day before they place their order?

Something that annoys me is a server not paying attention to what was ordered and not taking ownership of the mistake. If I order a drink and a glass of ice water, I expect to get what I ordered. I don't want the waiter to come back to my table and ask me twice what I ordered. WRITE IT DOWN if you don't have a good memory. And serve me what I ordered. Don't ask me when you get back to the table what I ordered. Number the items, make a game out of remembering who ordered what. Serve the right drinks or food to the right customer.

If your customer has ordered coffee, tea or an alcoholic drink to start off the meal, give them the option of ordering immediately or ask in a way that makes them feel like you care if they want to take some time before ordering. What's the rush? Are you going anywhere? Is there a line-up for the table? Even if there is, don't make your customer feel like they are in the fast food lane and have to pull out of the driveway.

I know we are not in Europe but in many ways, I wish we were. I believe Europeans have it right when it comes to their meal time. They eat slowly. They enjoy the event. They appreciate the leisure time spent around a table with friends and family. Good conversation and good food are nourishing to the soul and body. Remember the old saying, "Stop and smell the roses"? In a restaurant it's, "Stop and smell the aromas."

I hate being rushed. If I am in a hurry, I let the wait staff know this. If I am there to enjoy the meal, I let them know. I believe they appreciate it more than you can imagine. They know what you want and how you want it. A happy arrangement. Once they find out the appropriate tempo for each table, they can adjust their pace accordingly.

A casual check-in with the table is nice, but don't be annoying by checking too often. If you are given a time-frame, keep it in mind. If you are told to check back in five minutes, don't go back in two or ten minutes. Try to keep it around five minutes. If you see a drink glass empty, that might be a good time to check in with them even if it isn't the allotted time. People do like the fact that you are watching over them.

If your customer indicates that they are ready to order, take the time to discuss the menu with them, even if they are regular customers. This is when the server should mention the specials. Make sure the customer is aware of not only what the specials are and how much they cost, but any special descriptions about each item. It's always a good idea for your staff to taste the food they are serving. KNOW YOUR MENU. Be articulate, enthusiastic, and above all else--efficient.

Watch how the wait staff serves the drinks and food. This is a story in itself. It defines how you and your staff feel about the customer and their dining experience. It doesn't matter if you are a fast food or a 5-star restaurant. It all should be served with the same requirement--respect to the customer. Service is 50 percent of the dining experience. If you have bad service, it doesn't matter how good the food is.

I am appalled at how wait staff serve drinks and food. It doesn't take a Ph.D. to know that you don't ask your customer to serve the others at the table or to remember what they ordered and it definitely doesn't take a Ph.D. to see that a customer's needs are not being met.

It is a little more difficult to be served properly in a booth versus a table, but the same basic principles apply.

At Howard Johnson's (HoJo's), they had a lot of great rules about how to serve everything from a glass of water right through to dessert.

1. Serve water. Don't ask the customer if they want it. Everyone one should be served a glass of water unless they specifically decline it.

2. Drinks--water, soda, alcoholic, iced tea, or anything wet will sweat. Serve it with a coaster. Don't serve something that has spilled over on your tray without first wiping it with a clean napkin, then putting it on a coaster. Your customer doesn't like a messy table or spills on their clothes. I'm going to talk more about the messy table later.

3. Serve all drinks on the right side of the guest if possible. NEVER serve over another guest at a table. Walk around and serve it properly.

4. Ready to serve the appetizer? Ask if it is going to be shared and bring enough small plates and utensils for all.

5. Remove the appetizer and all dirty plates before you even think about asking if they are ready to order.

6. If they are ready, take the order, ask about refills on drinks and time your service.

7. If you offer rolls and butter with the meals, serve them with a bread plate for each guest. Put the bread basket in the center of the table if possible.

8. Now comes the tricky part. Train your staff to time the meal with the kitchen. Don't rush your customer through their salad time. Let them enjoy this part of the meal. Once they are done with the salad, remove the dirty plate. Freshen the table if need be. Ask if they need more bread. Show that you care.

9. When serving the main meal, use a tray to carry the plates. This insures that the meal can be served systematically. What do I mean by this? First serve the women in the group. If and only if the booth is so deep that the wait staff can't reach to place the meal in front of the person, they can

ask that it be passed. Otherwise, walk around the table and serve from the RIGHT side of the person. Always server from the right and remove from the left. Make note of their needs. Do they need more water, clean silverware or a napkin? Ask if they need anything before you walk away. It is very annoying to have been served and find that you didn't get what you ordered or you need something, like a fork.

10. Serving coffee, tea, water or anything else that needs to be refilled. I love to have my coffee poured from about three feet above the cup-- wrong. Pick up the cup and remove it from the table before you pour. I always have appreciated having a saucer. NEVER touch the rim of the cup or glass. I don't want your hands touching where my mouth has to go.

11. So now the parties at the table are eating. Give them some time and return with a smile to make sure that everything is going as expected. If they say that all is good, leave them alone until you see that everyone is done eating. Another one of my pet peeves is a waiter interrupting my meal multiple times. If it wanted to have dinner with them, I'd have invited them to the table.

12. NEVER and I mean NEVER remove plates from the table while others are still eating. It's rude. It makes me feel like I'm being rushed out the door. Remove all of the plates at the same time. Bring more water once the plates are removed and then ask if they are interested in anything else, such as dessert, coffee, after dinner drinks or just the check.

Here's another – NEVER, NEVER, EVER bring the check to the table while someone is still eating, unless they have emphatically requested it.

Part of the reason that I'm writing this book is because I was so furious about a time when we had barely started to eat our dinner. We were at a nice local restaurant that we used to frequent quite often. The restaurant wasn't full nor did it have a waiting line. The waitress was pleasant. She didn't seem like she was at the end of her shift, or was anxious for us to leave. However, this changed when she served our food. Let me back up a moment. I asked that we not be rushed. We were there to have a leisurely meal and needed to discuss some business opportunities.

We had taken just a few bites of our meals when she came to our table asking if we'd like dessert. Dessert, are you kidding? Our food had just been served. The next think I knew, she placed our check on the table. I saw red with this one. Needless to say, she didn't get the normal tip that we would have left and the next day the owner and I had a very long discussion about the fact that they should never allow this type of service.

It took us many months before we went back. I'm sorry we did. My husband and I were asked to go out to dinner with another couple. It was my cousin and her husband. She mentioned that she knew I wasn't particularly happy with this place but would we give it another try. I started out as a very pleasant Michigan summer evening. We were dining on their patio. We mentioned to the waitress that we were not in a hurry and would she give us some time before we ordered.

She ignored our request to give us time to enjoy our drinks. After being asked at least three times if we were ready to order, we suggested to her that when we were ready we would put all of the menus in one spot. Really?

Her next mistake was bringing the wrong meals to our table. Two out of the four were wrong. Once the correct meals arrived, we still needed her to bring a few things that were missing from the plates. UGH! How hard can it be to bring the right meals with everything on it to the right table? Then the same thing happened as before. Two different waitresses. Same place. Same service. I couldn't believe it. We were only half done with our meals when she asked us if we were going to order dessert. In my less than pleasant tone, I must admit, I asked her if she needed the table and if not would she at least allow us to finish our meals. Even if we wanted dessert or anything else, you can bet we weren't about to order it. Nor will I be going back to this place anytime soon. In fact, just because I like the owners, I will be giving them a copy of this book.

I hate it, (yes, that's a strong word) but I do hate it when a potentially good restaurant has issues like this in a small town. I love dining out locally. I really like supporting the local merchants but with service like this, I feel that they don't deserve the support of the people in the community.

8

The Ambiance

Noise. You may not notice it but your customer really does. A local new restaurant has a very clean, inviting and trendy atmosphere. The food is good and service is fine but you can't carry on a conversation because of the noise. I asked the waitress when we sat down if she could turn down the music volume. She asked if I was serious. Really? YES I was serious. We were out to dinner with friends and needed to have a serious conversation. There was no way we could hear each other. We were "out of there" and will be until they tone it down. I've tried so many times to ignore this but it seems to be getting worse. A restaurant is not a concert hall. It's a place to go and enjoy a good meal and your company.

Would you turn up the music so loud at home to the point that you can't talk at dinner? You have guests at the table to enjoy not only the meal but the company. If you can't hear what they are saying, then the meal is a flop. No matter how good the food might be, you couldn't enjoy the event and a meal is an event. Or should be. You'd never allow your teenager to get away with this. So why do YOU do it?

There are machines to handle noise if the building has a high ceiling that serves as an echo chamber. Yes, it's another thing to buy but it's worth it. Your customers will appreciate the thoughtfulness.

I remember as a child going out to dinner with my family and it was special. We'd go to all different types of restaurants but each time it was somewhere where we could enjoy the good food, service and conversations. Some of the places had soft music playing through speakers, some had juke boxes at the tables but they all had the levels turned down so that it didn't bother others and it didn't interfere with the meal.

My suggestion is for you to sit at one of your tables during a busy evening and try to talk to one of your customers. Is it possible? Can you hear them? Do you have to shout? If you do, then so does everyone else in the room. You're not at an indoor sporting arena, you're at a restaurant.

Do you really need televisions all over the room AND music playing? If I want to watch TV, I'll eat at home or in the bar area. Unless you operate a sports bar, it's not necessary. If you are going to the expense of providing a good dining area, good food and great service, don't take away from this by having blaring televisions trying to overpower the music, which also should be appropriate to the environment.

9

The Kitchen

We talked about a noisy dining area and how irritating it is to not be able to talk or hear the conversation at your table.

One other source of noise is the kitchen. When the staff opens the door can you hear all the racket going on in this area? Check it out and make some adjustments.

It might be fun to watch the chef cook if that's the way the restaurant is designed but it's not fun to hear him/her yell at the staff or the dishes clanking.

Is the door to your kitchen too close to the tables? Is there a way to rearrange that area or put up a wall to provide privacy? Give it some thought.

I love the TV show where the chef goes into the restaurant and shows the owner what's wrong with everything from the front to the back door. I guess I want to be that person now. I want to show you another area that I especially have concerns over--the kitchen.

Where do I start? Let's start with the chef or cook. The person cooking the food or overseeing the preparation of everything should at least be experienced. There's so much for that person to know and understand.

Allowing a chef free run of the kitchen can bankrupt you faster than any other part of the business. The margins are tight on food. Where you make your best margins, (and I don't need to tell you this), is on drinks. Most high end chefs understand that it's a partnership with the owners but they require complete control of the kitchen operations. That is fine, if you are confident in their abilities.

You as a business owner need to know the kitchen as much as anyone. You need to be able to take over flawlessly. Your ability to step in those shoes can make or break you. Without a doubt, you can serve a drink or a meal. You can wash dishes or mop a floor but can you cook? You don't need to be a certified chef but you do need to understand what it takes to be one and how the day-to-day operations work.

Allowing a chef free run of the kitchen can bankrupt you faster than any other part of the business. The margins are tight on food. Where you make your best margins, and I don't need to tell you this, is on drinks. Most high end chefs understand that it's a partnership with the owners but they require complete control of the kitchen operations. That is fine, if you are confident in their abilities.

If you are operating under a tight budget, then you need to help make some decisions on what is being ordered. Having too much food is worse than running out during rush hour. Running out can mean that it's a good item, but having to throw out food isn't an ideal situation. Planning takes a lot of thought. It's just like planning a family meal. You plan the number of ounces of meat, potatoes, veggies, etc. per person. I'll bet you don't purchase twice as much as needed. A little extra is fine just in case you have extra guests, or you want to use the leftovers. Have a plan in place and work on it constantly.

Another local place we used to go had the best calamari. We ordered it almost every time. All of a sudden it was removed from the menu. The waitress told us that it didn't sell so they removed it. They had to throw too much of it away. Hello! Maybe the chef was ordering too much or preparing too much in advance. Something this simple can be made up in small batches and cooked upon demand. I guess the owner wasn't a part of that thought process until it was too late.

Portions are very important to make a profit. Healthy portions are appreciated. Large portions are wasted. Easy economics. Even if you feel that your prices are right, maybe you be doing your guests a disservice by not offering the proper portion and making sure that it is prepared properly.

Now that we've talked about your role in the ordering and preparation of the food, let's talk about the kitchen's health.

Are your employees healthy? Are they aware of the local, state and federal rules of working in a kitchen? Are you checking on them periodically? Do you send them home when they are sick or do you demand that they stay and serve your guests while sneezing all over the plates? Seriously, I had pneumonia and was reprimanded because I called off on a Saturday night. It was an upscale restaurant in Warren, Ohio. It was one of the more popular places to dine in the area. I wasn't about to go to work sneezing, coughing and hacking all over the food and customers. It didn't matter to the owner. He was more concerned that he didn't have a warm body there to serve his guests.

Of course, I didn't go in to work. When I returned on that following Monday, I immediately told them that I no longer wanted to be employed at a place that not only had no regard for their staff but even less for their customers.

I look back at that time and I'm so proud of my actions. I knew I was doing the right thing even though I needed the job. You should be doing the same. Care for your staff but make sure that they respect your wishes as well. Help keep them healthy.

One of the ways to keep everyone to stay healthy is to keep the sick at bay. I've been the recipient of salmonella from a well-known fast food chain. I ate a fish sandwich with tainted mayonnaise. Needless to say, I was one sick individual. My son, who was 18 months old at the time, contracted it from me. I ended up in the hospital for a week. Our son was more fortunate.

I asked the manager how this could have happened. One possibility was that an employee had the disease. It was transmitted to me through the mayo. Somehow, the germ got into the container. Not a good thing to happen to anyone.

Now let's look around the kitchen. When was the last time you thoroughly cleaned everything? Have you totally cleaned this room each week? Do you sanitize everything, every day? Have you moved the shelving in the freezer or do you just wipe around the containers? Do you have a cleaning policy and do you make sure that it is followed? What does the health board think about your facility?

A local sports bar style restaurant in my hometown was closed by the health board. It looked O.K. when you walked in. After all it's a sports bar. I thought the food was disgusting but more importantly, the kitchen was found to be full of pure filth. The management said that they were going to clean it. After being open for two years, you would think they knew it needed to be cleaned.

I was there one night after a meeting with some friends. I ordered stuffed potato skins. Immediately I told the waitress that they tasted moldy. First of all, I have a really great sense of taste. Secondly, she argued with me that they couldn't be and last of all she still charged me for them. Well guess what? The health board recognized that they were serving outdated, spoiled and dirty food and closed them for good. O.K., enough about that place.

There's a time limit on all fresh and frozen food. Be aware of dates. Don't serve outdated food and don't get to a point where you have to throw it out. That's money thrown away.

One of my first jobs in manufacturing was working for a company that manufactured floor matting. I was part of the design team. The product was an interlocking, nonslip system. For the first two years of working on this project, my job was to install the matting in kitchens, bars, and entrance ways. Our goal was to produce a product that would provide not only anti-fatigue features and benefits but a slip proof surface. One of the side benefits was that the liquids and debris fell between the strips and out of the way. Boy did it ever help. When the matting was removed it was easy to see how much was dropped each shift, and therefore not tracked into other parts of the kitchen, making it more safe for the chef/cook to work. Giving them an anti-fatigue surface also prevented them from tired, aching feet and from slipping on the wet or greasy floor, which was so appreciated by the staff. This product was also designed to go through the dishwasher each night to keep it sanitary. Can you say this about your cooking area? Are you providing your staff with a safe and comfortable work space? You should, because they are a very important piece of the pie.

Back to the idea of your customer being able to see in your kitchen. What's their impression?

Another story. There's a tavern we used to go to where the entrances are at the front and back of the building. Neither entrance is remotely clean I must add. The back entrance has you walk past the kitchen. I'm surprised by how disorganized and utterly filthy it is. I know the owner but I can't give her a break on this one. I really don't want to see in the kitchen. I know it's hard to keep it perfect but you can keep it organized and clean. Plus, I don't understand the need to operate a kitchen with the doors open. There are other health issues to consider. You don't need the outside dirt and germs entering this area. Oh and did I mention that the entrance carpeting is disgustingly dirty. What a first impression!

Keep the kitchen clean! Demand this of the staff. It actually helps them. Remember when your mother or teacher told you to make sure your things were organized and your room was clean? Same concept in the kitchen. Your mother knew where to find her supplies and spices. She also made sure that her work area was clean. She'd never prepare a meal in a dirty kitchen. Why would you?

How often do you require your staff to open and refresh their supply containers? How often do you check temperatures of food that isn't in the refrigerator or cooler? Do you have a policy and follow it? Give this a lot of thought. One case of salmonella or e-coli will close your doors--permanently.

10

The Food

We've talked about your role in the kitchen and how to maintain the staff and environment. Now let's talk about the food you serve.

Your Menu

Who sets your menu? Are you involved? How many times per year do you change it?

Believe me when I say that even your regular customer who loves one of your entrées may like to try something else. Do you offer specials? Keep them coming back with healthy and tasty meals.

The trend or movement in the restaurant industry is to offer healthy, tasty and new entrees. Fresh food, gluten-free, no GMO, light or organic. You can do this with so many recipes without making major changes to your menu. People are trying to stay healthy and live longer healthier lives. Fried, greasy, heavy food are O.K. occasionally but light, healthy meals are more desirable. Offer a fresh veggie plate as an appetizer. Don't forget the Ranch Dip. Again, a healthy addition to the menu.

Maybe you've noticed that more people do not want the rolls or potatoes. More are going for the fresh style meals. There's a reason--carbs, sugar and calories. Yet they want a tasty, filling meal.

Take a look at the menus of other restaurants similar to yours. You can easily do this online. Choose a few new items that look like something your clientele will order. Keep a theme to your menu unless you run a home-cooked family style restaurant that offers a variety of items. Most good restaurants keep to a theme. Italian, Chinese, French, etc.

If you watch your menu items and the trend of the ordering, you will see which ones are popular and what you need to remove. Portions are important when deciding what to serve and they affect your bottom line.

One more reminder--having an item on the menu that no one really wants to buy any longer is wasting food--throwing money down the drain.

Let's take a little bit of time to discuss the fundamentals of a meal. Throw the basic food groups out the window! People want meals that are appealing, healthy and filling. However, there are still some comfort foods that will always remain on the menu and are favorites of your customers.

If you are smart, you will actually eat your own food. Or have a secret diner come in periodically to test it. Surprisingly your staff can, without cause, start to slip on the quality and your customers will notice.

Recently I ordered coconut shrimp. Wow, was I surprised at the difference! I asked if they had hired a new chef. The improvement was amazing.

The same thing can happen the other way. If your customer is familiar with a certain menu item and it doesn't meet their expectations, then there is a problem in the kitchen. They may not say anything, just not come back. It's worse if they do say something--to their friends. Taste your meals regularly and without bias.

71

Train your staff to ask if they notice that someone has left most of their meal on the plate. Perhaps it wasn't what they were expecting. Perhaps it really isn't prepared per the description. The customer may be willing to accept it as a bad dinner one time but not twice.

We were at a well-known resort in Colorado Springs for our anniversary. We chose one of their restaurants that had great reviews and a very different style menu. We love to eat new things. I chose a lamb stew. When it arrived, my first impression was that I was eating wallpaper paste. "Maybe I don't really like lamb that much," I thought. However, our waiter noticed that I wasn't eating it. I simply said that it wasn't my favorite thing and perhaps I shouldn't have ordered it. Not his fault. Not the chef's fault (maybe it was). The manager came over in a few minutes and insisted that he get me something else. I declined. It was an unusual meal anyway. I took a chance on it. Not their fault that I didn't like it. BUT they had a policy that if a customer doesn't like their meal and it was obvious they weren't eating it, they didn't have to pay for it. Impressed? You bet I was. I would go back there and give it a second try. My husband had the salmon that was amazing.

11

Different Types of Establishments

I mentioned earlier that how you train and serve your clientele depends on your type of establishment. Not many things need to be handled differently, but here are a few examples of some differences.

Food Truck
This type of food service is different from sit-down service. Your priority is great food in a hurry. Your work space is limited. However, that doesn't mean that you can get away with a lower level of service and quality. You need to pay attention to your work space. Approach your customer as if they are the most important person in your life. In some respects they are. Your customer can

see your every move. The customer behind the one you are waiting on can see and hear everything. Clean counters, clean clothes, clean everything is important.

You don't need to worry about a clean floor for them to walk on, a clean table (unless you are providing them) or fine china. You're most likely serving their food in paper wrapping and paper tubs--perfect for the type of food and the way you serve it. Just make sure these items are clean. Keep the bugs at bay. Keep yourself and your staff neat and clean. Keeping your surrounding work area clean is a must.

Truck Stop/Diner
A truck stop, also known as a transport café and as a travel center by major chains in the United States, is a common facility which provides refueling, rest (parking) and often serves ready-made food to all types of travelers. Truck stops are usually located on or near busy roads.

Drivers provide an essential service to industrialized societies by transporting finished goods and raw materials over land, typically to and from manufacturing plants, retail distribution centers, and stores. These drivers are not always treated with the respect they deserve. They deserve the same benefits as someone who is paying $$$$ for a meal. They don't expect linen and china on the table but they do expect a clean environment, safe food and a tasty meal.

Why do the operators of these establishments treat them so poorly? Truck stops/diners are for the most part the worst places to eat. With a large customer turnover, it is a challenge to keep the facility clean, BUT NOT IMPOSSIBLE.

Family Diner
Taking your family out for dinner is an expensive venture. You want a good meal at a reasonable price. Diners can and should have the feel of a cozy dining room. The menu is normally more like home cooking-- pot roast, mashed potatoes, homemade rolls--get the picture? Families love comfort food and this is the type of place they look for when in the mood for a home cooked meal.

We were traveling through Nebraska when we decided to stop for something light to eat. Tired and hungry, we pulled off at an unknown exit. There was a really cute barn-looking café that looked too interesting not to explore. It was a newer building with one side housing a café and the other side a gift/antique shop. What a cute place. But the best part was the amazing food. I have never had a better cup of coffee or soup (other than my own) in this type of restaurant. Not only was it good, but the owner came to our table to meet us and make sure we were happy. What a great guy. He actually cared about two tired travelers who possibly will never return. We tried on several other occasions but he was not open for business when we were going through the area. What a shame. I wanted to try it again to make sure it was as good as I remembered.

Fast Food

This is a necessary evil in the restaurant industry. Fast food isn't always fast and it definitely isn't good. Why? It used to be. When McDonalds and Arby's opened, they served great sandwiches, amazing fries and delicious shakes. Many of the other older chains are gone. Why? Where did they go wrong? One reason is that they lost touch with their customer base. No longer does the customer expect much from them. They accept dirty floors, counters and cooking areas. Lack of respect for the consumer shows in the way restaurant employees treat them. Lack of training shows as well. I haven't been to a fast food establishment in the past few years that has gotten the order right and shown actual concern for me.

Buffet/Cafeteria
A buffet is a system of serving meals in which food is placed in a public area where the diners generally serve themselves.

It is also a place where you can eat all you want and have a variety to choose from all for one price. What you really get for your money might not be what you expect. Buffets have a reputation for not serving the best quality food or being the cleanest places. The food isn't prepared properly. The staff allows it to stay on the board too long and the serving area always seems to be a total mess.

The staff must be trained differently than a server in other types of food service. They need to have guidelines on the length of time food is allowed to stay on the board. They need to keep food at the right temperatures whether they are cold or hot, and keep food safe from the environment. Shielding the food from human germs is a big issue. No one wants to eat something that another person has touched or coughed on. Cleanliness is even more essential in a place like this.

Restaurant Chain
Casual dining. Faster, easier meals. Not a lot of frills.

A chain can be run with consistency. If you recall, I mentioned Howard Johnsons in the beginning of this book? This is a great example of how to run a restaurant. The training was phenomenal, and stays with you for the rest of your life.

A chain restaurant has the opportunity of setting the pace for every type of eating establishment. It can raise the bar on good food, great service, reasonable prices and of course, a clean enjoyable environment.

Bar/Grill

This is a place you can grab a drink and what I call "bar food," such as pizza, burgers, and fries. There's nothing special on the menu and it is normally fried food cooked by less than experienced individuals. Bar food doesn't need to be much. But it DOES need to be good. However, you can up your game and change the menu to make it the reason that your guests come back. Serving interesting and delicious meals at a bar with a great drink--sometimes it doesn't get any better than this.

The environment sets the tone. Clean, friendly staff, good food and you have a winner.

Independent Dining/Owner-Operated

These establishments have more of an upscale atmosphere. They normally have linen table coverings of some sort and better silver/dishes as well as trained staff and professional chefs. This is a more leisurely-timed meal, not where you are rushed through each course.

So this is where it hits home more than any others. You the owner/manager have complete control over how your operation is run. Take a real look at your restaurant now and see what changes you can make.

Five Star Dining

Five Star dining includes fine china, linen table coverings, proper matching silver and trained staff. Even this level of dining has its problems. Remember, I said that I have worked in many of these types of places. They are not always the cleanest or most efficiently run places. Every business has the same problems--servers quitting, moody chefs, janitorial crew missing the dirt, food spoilage and all of the rest of the usual problems.

12

Improve Operations to Satisfy Your Customers

What does it take to make you satisfied? What impresses you? Why do you return to a certain retail store or maybe even another restaurant? Think about this. What brings customers back to your place more than anything is that THEY LEFT SATISFIED. They had a great experience all the way around, and they shared that information with others.

With all the media coverage available today, it's so important that you make sure every customer is satisfied. It doesn't matter what type of establishment you have, once a bad report has been shared with others, i.e., on Facebook or Twitter, it's hard to recover from this.

Recently in my home town, two angry women posted on Facebook that they had food poisoning from a local casual dining place and the other posted how awful her experience was at a local independently owned more upscale establishment. Both later apologized publicly that they jumped to conclusions about their posts. Too little too late. The word of doubt was out there. The facts were shared with hundreds. How many of them read the rebuttals? I for one have had the same experience at the second one and mentioned it earlier in this book. Now, I'm not so sure that it will ever get resolved. How many others feel the same way? They lost my satisfaction rating.

What can you do to improve? How can you make your place stand out?

It's time to face reality about what you need to do.

1. Look at your building. How does it look?

2. What does your entry look like?

3. Get more out of your employees. Is your staff happy, clean and friendly? Do a little research on this area and fast. Weed out the dead weight. Don't keep negative staff.

4. How do you train your staff? Are they following your lead? Are you a good leader?

5. Can you eat off of the floor in your kitchen? I'll bet you wouldn't.

6. How do you control your expenses? Hire a consultant to work with you.

7. Do you know your customers and what they want/expect from you? Get to know them. This is time well spent.

8. Are you serving good food? Are you changing your menu frequently? Do you offer specials to keep people coming back? Ask your staff and customers what they like. Listen to them.

9. Are you available to meet and greet your customers? They are YOUR customers and your income.

10. What are you doing right? You must be doing something right or you wouldn't have your doors open. If you specialize in a cuisine and it's good, toot your horn. Publish positive things about it. Brag a little. It's good for you.

13

Let's Sum it up

Hopefully by now are you asking yourself: Am I doing all of these things? Am I doing any of these things?" What areas do I need to see improvement? Why didn't I see this before?

Don't fool yourself and say that it's the economy that's affecting your business. Ask yourself some of the hard questions, like: Could it be my servers that are running off my customers? Is it the quality of the food? Is the environment pleasing and clean?

It's not the economy like some would like to say. Look around at the lines at other restaurants. If you have an empty parking lot, it's not because you're having a bad day, it's because of bad service, bad food, dirty environment or all of the above. Prices don't seem to matter as much in this present economy. People are willing to pay for a good meal and good service.

I hope that in some way, I was able to open your eyes to a new brighter future. The reason I wanted to share this with you is that I want you to get more out of your business. I want to be able to go anywhere for a meal and feel satisfied that I chose the right place no matter where I am. This is a universal problem. It's an ongoing issue that needs to be addressed. It can start with you, the owner, the manager, the server, the chef, the busser, the janitor or whatever your title may be.

One simple yet very important thing is a warm "goodbye and thank you." This makes the customer feel like they were truly appreciated and that the staff would like them to come back--SOON and often.

www.ingramcontent.com/pod-product-compliance
Lightning Source LLC
Chambersburg PA
CBHW060639210326
41520CB00010B/1668